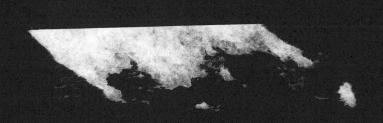

ANIMALS UNDER THREAT

KOALA

IN DANGER OF EXTINCTION!

Carol Inskipp

Heinemann
LIBRARY

www.heinemann.co.uk/library
Visit our website to find out more information about **Heinemann Library** books.

To order:
☎ Phone 44 (0) 1865 888066
🖹 Send a fax to 44 (0) 1865 314091
💻 Visit the Heinemann Bookshop at www.heinemann.co.uk/library to browse our catalogue and order online.

First published in Great Britain by Heinemann Library, Halley Court, Jordan Hill, Oxford OX2 8EJ, part of Harcourt Education.
Heinemann is a registered trademark of Harcourt Education Ltd.

Editorial: Sarah Jameson, Nicole Irving and Louise Galpine
Design: Ian Winton and Jo Malivoire
Picture Research: Laura Durman
Production: Camilla Smith
Illustration: Stefan Chabluk

Originated by Dot Gradations Ltd
Printed in China by WKT Company Limited

ISBN 0 431 18906 4
09 08 07 06 05
10 9 8 7 6 5 4 3 2 1

British Library Cataloguing in Publication Data
Inskipp, Carol
Koala - (Animals under threat)
599.2'5
A full catalogue record for this book is available from the British Library.

Acknowledgements
The publishers would like to thank the following for permission to reproduce photographs: Auscape pp. **20** (Jean-Paul Ferrero), **21** (Wayne Lawler), **27** (Jean-Paul Ferrero), **35** (Jean-Paul Ferrero); Australian Koala Foundation, www.savethekoala.com pp. **11** (Phillip Wright), **18**, **29**, **30**, **32** (Renee Sternberg), **33** (Gary Steer), **37** (M. Dalu), **42** (Jo Knights); Bruce Coleman Collection pp. **15** (John Cancalosi), **19** (John Cancalosi), **22** (David Austen), **34** (John Cancalosi), **38** (Staffan Widstrand); Bruce Coleman Inc. p. **4**; CORBIS pp. **24** (Kennan Ward), **39** (Robert Garvey), **40**, **41** (Steve Kaufman), **43** (Neil Rabinowitz), cover header and background image; FLPA p. **13** (Gerard Lacz); NHPA pp. **5** (T Kitchin & V Hurst), **10** (ANT), **14** (Gerard Lacz), **16** (Ann & Steve Toon), **36** (ANT); OSF pp. **12** (Kathie Atkinson), **25** (Roger Brown), **31** (Kathie Atkinson); John Oxley Library pp. **6** (neg. no. 18937), **7** (neg. no. 38267); Dick Roberts, Nelson, New Zealand pp. **9**, **23**; State Library of South Australia, B 49818 p. **26**.

Cover photograph reproduced with permission of NHPA / John Shaw.

The publishers would like to thank Michael Chinery and the Australian Koala Foundation for their assistance in the preparation of this book.

Contents

Words printed in the text in bold, **like this**, are explained in the Glossary.

Meet the koala

Many people think koalas look like bears because they have round bodies, big ears and broad, flat noses. Although the koala's scientific name is *Phascolarctos cinereus*, which means 'ash-grey, pouched bear', they are not related to the bear family at all! Like bears, they are **mammals** and feed their young on milk. Unlike bears, koalas belong to a very special group of mammals called **marsupials**.

Wild koalas are found only in Australia. They live in — and feed on — eucalyptus, or gum trees, which have grown in Australia for millions of years. Koalas have thick fur that is mostly white on the underside and grey on the rest of the body. The fur looks soft, but it feels quite rough, like sheep's wool.

Not so cuddly

Although koalas may look fluffy and are normally very gentle, they have very sharp teeth and claws. They can give a nasty bite if frightened.

Koalas are one of Australia's most well-known animals. They spend most of their time in the branches of eucalyptus trees.

▶

Marsupials are a varied group of animals. The Virginia opossum is North America's only marsupial. Like the koala, the female opossum has a pouch in which her young develop.

What is a marsupial?

Since early European explorers first encountered them in Australia, marsupials have fascinated people all over the world. The word marsupial comes from the Latin *marsupium*, meaning 'pouch'. Marsupials give birth to tiny, under-developed young. After birth, the infants grow up outside their mother's body, usually in a pouch. Many Australian mammals are marsupials: the largest is the human-sized red kangaroo, and the smallest is the shrew-like ningaui that can fit into a human hand. Marsupials live in a wide range of **habitats**, from **rainforests** and mountains to deserts. Some, like the marsupial mole, eat insects; some, like kangaroos and wallabies, eat leaves and grass; others like the sugar glider, feed on nectar and tree sap. There are a few meat-eating marsupials such as the fierce Tasmanian devil. There are also marsupials in Papua New Guinea and parts of Indonesia, and a few in North, South and Central America.

Why are Koalas threatened?

Today, the number of koalas throughout much of Australia is falling and they are already becoming **extinct** in some places. The main threat to them is the loss of their habitat. They depend upon certain types of eucalyptus woodland to survive, but these are getting smaller and smaller in size. This is because humans have cleared away vast areas of **bush** for farming, houses, roads and factories. The situation is made worse by bushfires and the gradual loss of trees, known as tree dieback, caused by harmful changes in the **environment**. Koalas living in or near towns are also in danger from domestic dogs which often attack and kill them, and many koalas are run over by cars.

The **ancestors** of today's koalas probably lived in the **rainforests** that once covered much of Australia. Scientists have found **fossil** remains of koala-like animals that are around 25 million years old. Over a long period of time, Australia's climate gradually became drier. Eucalyptus trees began to grow and koalas **evolved** to live alongside them.

Humans and koalas

Aboriginal people were the first to live in Australia and probably arrived around 60,000 years ago. Although some tribes killed koalas for food, it is thought that these animals were still very common when the first Europeans arrived in Australia in 1788.

In the 19th century large numbers of people came from Europe to settle in Australia, and they began to cut down the **native** forest to make way for their farmland and human settlements. As well as destroying the koala's **habitat**, the settlers started to kill them for their fur.

What's in a name?

The various Aboriginal tribes had many different names for the koala, among them the colo, koolah, boorabee, karbor, kaola and koolewong! The name 'koala' means 'no drink' in one of the Aboriginal languages.

The truck in this photograph is piled high with more than 3500 rolled-up koala skins. These koalas, and many more, were killed by fur hunters in the space of just one month in Queensland in 1927.

European settlers cleared large areas of woodland so they could farm the land. They used the wood to build farmhouses and make fences, carts and farm tools. This photograph was taken around 1887 near Brisbane in Queensland.

The fur trade had a devastating effect on koala **populations**. In the late 19th and early 20th centuries millions of koalas were killed. Most skins were exported to Europe and the USA. This large-scale slaughter of koalas caused a major public outcry. By the end of the 1930s, koalas were declared a protected **species** and deliberate killing of koalas became illegal. By this time they had become **extinct** in the state of South Australia and their numbers were massively reduced in other places. Although the koala was finally given some protection, laws were not brought in at that time to protect the eucalyptus trees that the koalas need for food and shelter.

Australia's wildlife under pressure

Australia is home to over a million species of plants and animals. Because the country has been isolated for millions of years, many of its species are found nowhere else on Earth. The koala, duck-billed platypus, wombat and emu are some of the very unusual animals that are unique to Australia. The Australian climate is often extreme. Over much of the country the rainfall is very low, with most rain falling on coastal areas. The south has cool, wet winters and hot, dry summers. In the north the climate is **tropical**. Like the koala that eats mainly eucalyptus leaves, many of Australia's animals have very specialized **diets**. This means they are at great risk from the changes taking place in their habitats today. Over 1400 species are now considered threatened in Australia.

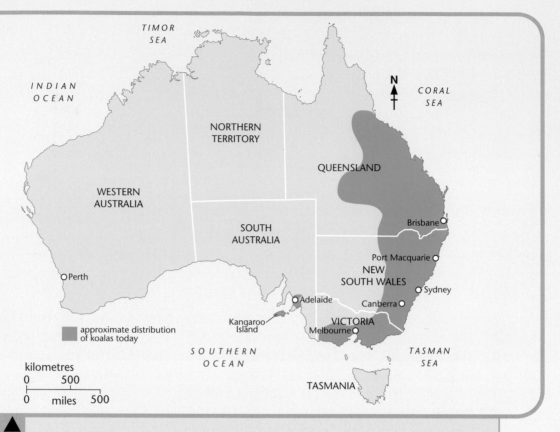

TIMOR SEA

INDIAN OCEAN

N

CORAL SEA

NORTHERN TERRITORY

QUEENSLAND

WESTERN AUSTRALIA

Brisbane

SOUTH AUSTRALIA

Port Macquarie

NEW SOUTH WALES

○Perth

Sydney

○Adelaide

Canberra○

Kangaroo Island

VICTORIA

Melbourne○

approximate distribution of koalas today

SOUTHERN OCEAN

TASMAN SEA

kilometres
0   500

0   miles   500

TASMANIA

This map shows the koala's distribution in Australia today. Koalas are not distributed evenly, but are found in sometimes widely separated areas.

Fossil remains of koalas have been found in western Australia, central South Australia and north-west Queensland. These are areas where koalas can't live today, because the climate is too dry. Although we do not know the exact **distribution** of koalas before the Europeans arrived, we do know that eucalyptus forests once covered much of eastern Australia. These forests would have provided vast areas of ideal **habitat** for koalas. There is no doubt that these animals used to live over a much greater part of Australia than they do today.

Nowadays, koalas live in the eastern and some southern parts of Australia. They live from Queensland in the north, down through coastal and inland areas of New South Wales and Victoria to South Australia. There is also a population of koalas on Kangaroo Island, which lies just off the south coast.

South-east Queensland is home to one of the largest koala **populations** by far. Unfortunately, this part of Australia with its fertile soils also has the fastest growing human population. Here expanding towns and cities are threatening the koala's remaining habitat. Some koalas have been re-**introduced** into South Australia and Victoria to start new populations, replacing those lost by hunting for the fur trade. Although this was meant to help koalas, re-introduction has led to many problems for them in these areas.

How many koalas?

When Europeans first arrived in Australia in the 18th century there were possibly 10 million or more koalas. In the two centuries since then the population has fallen dramatically. Scientists do not always agree on the current size of the koala population although some believe the total number is somewhere between 100,000 and 200,000 animals.

Disease and koalas

Diseases are a natural part of life for koalas. One common disease called chlamydia has been present in koala populations for many years. Scientists believe that it could act as a natural population control. This means that it is generally harmless in healthy koalas that have plenty of food and shelter, but it affects weaker animals or those that are under stress. Coping with loss of habitat and other difficulties can cause stress or upset in animals. Chlamydia disease is occurring more frequently in koalas today because they are under more stress. The disease causes various problems including eye and lung infections. It causes some of the weaker animals to die, leaving the stronger ones to continue breeding.

Huge areas of koala habitat have now been cleared away. Here trees have been cut down to make way for industry and housebuilding south of Sydney. You can see the remaining woodland on the hills in the distance.

Koalas and the eucalyptus tree

Eucalyptus trees, or eucalypts, grow over much of Australia. There are well over 600 different **species** and almost all of them are **native** to Australia. Most are found in forests and woodlands in areas with higher rainfall, although almost every **habitat** except the extremely wet or extremely dry has one or more species. The trees vary in appearance from short bushes to elegant trees over 100 metres tall.

One of the most unusual things about eucalypts is their amazing powers of recovery after a fire. The tree produces new shoots from buds on the trunk and main branches, or from large, swollen stems underground or at the base of the tree, called **lignotubers**.

A home for wildlife

Many native plants and animals live only in eucalyptus woodlands. Koalas are very choosy about their habitat, and will only live in an area if their favourite species of eucalypt are growing there. The greater glider, ringtail possum and koala are the only **mammals** that can live on a **diet** of eucalyptus leaves.

Eucalyptus trees like these are well suited to the Australian climate. They don't lose all their leaves, even in a bad drought, so they provide food and shelter for koalas all year round. Most eucalypts live for 300 years or more, and a few may reach 1000 years of age.

Eucalyptus woodlands are fast disappearing in Australia. Koalas like this one depend on eucalpyts for their food and shelter.

A flowering eucalypt is a gathering place for many animals that depend on its nectar or pollen for at least part of their diet. Bats, parrots, honeyeaters and many different sorts of insects are just some of the animals that live in eucalyptus woodlands, alongside koalas. The trees themselves depend upon many of their visitors to **pollinate** their flowers so they can make seeds for future years. Eucalyptus tree hollows also provide roosting and nesting places for animals such as the ringtail possum and various birds.

Some koala favourites

These are the common names of some of the koala's favourite types of eucalypts:
- river red gum
- yellow box
- tallowwood
- small-leafed peppermint
- drooping red gum
- grey gum
- manna gum.

Problems with paper

The woodchip industry is big business in Australia today. Trees, including eucalypts and other native species, are chopped down to make woodchips which are then turned into paper (eucalypts make especially fine, smooth writing paper) as well as a building material called chipboard. Clearing forests for this purpose is one of the many threats to koala habitat today.

Useful trees

Aborigines discovered that eucalyptus roots contained water which they could drink when they were thirsty. They also found out that the oil in eucalyptus leaves was a useful medicine. Today eucalyptus oil is used to treat many ailments including coughs, colds, asthma and problems with the muscles and joints. It is good for keeping insects away too.

Adaptable koalas

It is generally thought that there are two types, or **subspecies**, of koala: the northern koala, found in Queensland and northern New South Wales, and the southern koala from Victoria, South Australia and southern New South Wales. The southern koala is usually larger than the northern koala, and has longer, thicker and more brownish fur. These differences are probably **adaptations** to different temperatures: in the north the climate is warm but in the south it is much colder and snow can fall in some areas in winter.

How large are koalas?

Northern and southern koalas differ in size and weight. These figures show the average adult size and weight for males and females of both subspecies:

	Length	Weight
southern koala adult male	78 cm	12 kg
southern koala adult female	72 cm	8.5 kg
northern koala adult male	70.5 cm	6.5 kg
northern koala adult female	64 cm	5 kg

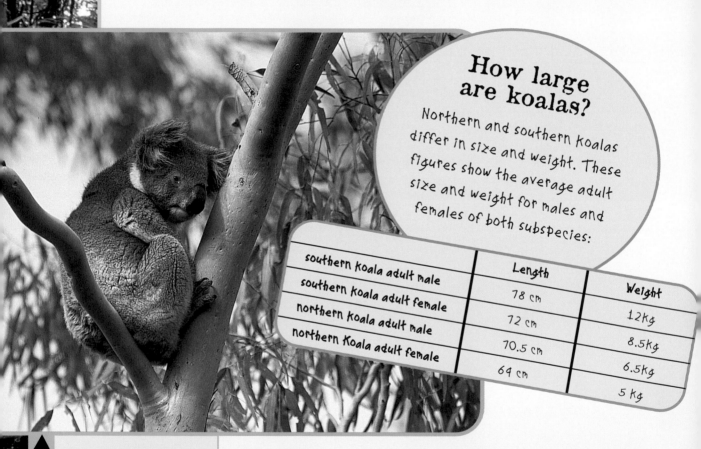

Koalas spend a large part of their day sleeping or resting in the branches. On the rump the fur is especially thick, making a useful cushion to sit on.

Koalas have dense coats that prevent them from becoming too hot or too cold, so they do not need to build nests or take shelter in tree holes. In wet weather the fur, which is particularly thick on the head and shoulders, acts like a raincoat, keeping the koalas dry. As koalas are not able to lose heat by sweating, they cool themselves down by stretching out in the shade of the trees and dangling their limbs down. In colder weather they curl up into a ball to keep in their body heat.

Koala signs

Claw marks or scratches on tree trunks are a good sign of regular use by koalas. These are made by the animals jumping up from the ground and catching their front claws on the bark. Another sign that koalas are present is their droppings at the base of trees. These are long and rounded in shape, about the size of an olive stone and green to brown in colour. They often have a eucalyptus smell if crushed.

Life in the trees

Koalas are well adapted to life in trees. A good sense of balance and a broad bottom help make them more stable while sitting or resting on branches. They are excellent climbers and have special hands and feet to help them. Rough paw pads and long, sharp claws give them a good grip on tree trunks and branches. Long, strong arms and legs support their weight. Their front paws have a large gap between the first and second finger, rather like our thumb and fingers. This helps them grip branches more easily.

A large nose means that koalas can detect differences in smell between the many different types of eucalyptus leaves. This is important as it helps koalas to choose the best leaves. A keen sense of smell also means they can pick up the scent warnings left on trees by other koalas.

With their strong arms and legs, flexible paws and very sharp claws, koalas can move around trees with ease.

Diet and feeding

Koalas are well-known for being very selective about their **diet**. They eat mainly eucalyptus leaves, and must have these to survive, although they do like a change of food now and again. Sometimes they also eat leaves from other trees, such as wattle or tea tree. Koalas don't normally need to drink. Instead they get moisture from the leaves they eat and from rainwater or dew that collects on them. They can drink if they need to, though, such as in times of drought.

A leafy diet

Adult koalas can munch through around 500 grams of eucalyptus leaves each day and sometimes more. These leaves are very high in **fibre** but low in **nutrients**. They also contain poisonous chemicals called **toxins** that scientists think help to protect the trees against leaf-eating pests, such as insects. Trees that grow on poor soils may have more toxins than those growing on good soils and the leaves themselves can also contain increased amounts of toxins at certain times of the year. Koalas often avoid eating leaves from eucalyptus trees under these circumstances.

Fussy feeders

Koalas eat leaves from only a few of the 600 or more **species** of eucalypt that grow in Australia. They will often eat leaves from just two or three favoured species, and sometimes the leaves from only one. The trees that koalas prefer may also vary with the season. Having a restricted diet like this causes big problems for koalas when their favourite food source is under threat or in short supply.

Eucalyptus leaves do not have many nutrients so koalas have to eat a lot of them to stay strong and healthy.

Koalas are careful about which eucalyptus leaves they eat and often give them a good sniff first to find out if they are suitable.

Special **adaptations** help koalas cope with their diet of leaves. Very slow body processes allow koalas to keep the food they eat inside their **digestive system** for a longer time than most animals. This means they can absorb as many nutrients as possible from it. They can also break down the toxins in the leaves into harmless chemicals. A special organ in their digestive system, called the caecum, contains millions of **bacteria** that break down the large amounts of leaf fibre into substances that are easier to absorb. Compared to its body size, the koala's caecum is larger than that of any other **mammal**.

Koala teeth

Koalas have teeth that are well adapted to deal with their diet of tough leaves. Sharp front teeth nip the leaves from the tree and special back teeth grind them up. A gap between the front and back teeth allows the tongue to move a mass of leaves around in the mouth more easily when chewing. Cheek pouches in their mouth allow food to be stored unchewed if the koalas have to move quickly to a safer place.

Smelly koalas

Some people say that koalas smell like cough drops because of their diet of eucalyptus leaves!

Koala behaviour

Koalas are mainly **nocturnal** animals, which means they are more active at night. The air is cooler at this time, so koalas lose less valuable moisture than they would during hot daylight hours. Moving around is also less tiring when it is cooler. Koalas spend eighteen to twenty hours each day resting and sleeping in trees. They only come to the ground when moving from one tree to another. When they are not sleeping, koalas are often eating. They spend less than 1 per cent of their day in other activities, such as grooming, travelling between trees or finding a mate.

Koalas have an excellent sense of balance and this dozing koala looks very comfortable perched in the fork of a tree.

Because koalas move around so slowly and sleep so much, some people think they are drugged by eating eucalyptus leaves, but this is not true. Koalas have a peaceful, sleepy lifestyle because they need to use as little energy as possible in order to survive. This is because their **diet** is low in **nutrients** and because they store little or no fat on their bodies to use as a source of energy. The amount of food they eat each day provides them with about as much energy as one bowl of breakfast cereal does for us!

This pie chart shows the proportion of time that koalas spend on different activities during a typical day. They spend a huge amount of time just sleeping or resting to save energy.

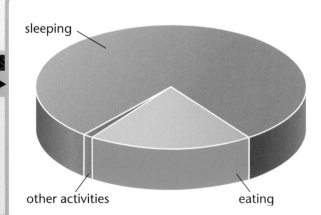

sleeping

other activities

eating

This is a simplified diagram showing how koala home ranges overlap with each other. M1 is the most powerful male in the group and his home range is the largest of all. Although koalas like to live on their own, they need to be near other koalas in their group.

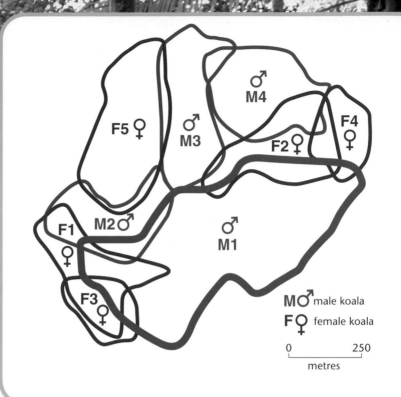

F5 ♀ M3 ♂ M4 ♂ F2 ♀ F4 ♀

F1 ♀ M2 ♂ M1 ♂

F3 ♀

M♂ male koala
F♀ female koala

0   250
metres

The home range

Although koalas belong to a group, they live in their own trees and normally only interact with each other during the breeding season. Koalas do not wander aimlessly about the **bush**. Each koala lives and moves within its own **territory** — its **home range**. These can be as little as a few hectares in size to well over 100 hectares. The size of the home range depends on the number of suitable trees in it. Where there are fewer suitable trees, the home ranges are generally larger in size.

The home ranges of koalas in a group usually overlap so the animals can meet up in the breeding season. Within its home range, the koala will regularly use the same trees. These are called its home trees. Koalas mark out their ranges by scratching their home trees and leaving their scent on them. Koalas usually stay in their home range for life unless there is disturbance to the **habitat**.

Bellows and squeaks

Koalas use a wide range of sounds to communicate with each other. Males have a deep, grunting bellow. Females bellow too, but less often than males. Mothers and young hum, murmur and squeak to each other as well as gently grunting to express bad feeling. If very upset, koalas utter a frightening cry that sounds like a baby screaming.

Koalas breed between September and March, which is summer in Australia. They are more active at this time of year and the males are noisier than usual. The koala's breeding rate is fairly low: females usually produce only one young each year — twins are rare. Some females give birth only every two or three years depending on their age and the quality of their **habitat**.

Growing up

As with other **marsupials**, a young koala is called a joey. When it is born the joey is very tiny, at around just two centimetres long. It weighs less than one gram (about the weight of a few grains of rice), has no hair and looks like a pink jelly bean!

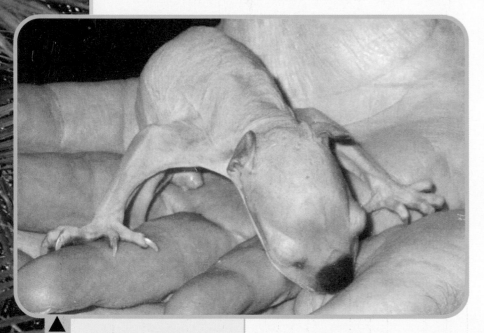

The newborn joey cannot see or hear, but its strong limbs, keen sense of smell and touch and built-in sense of direction help it to climb to its mother's pouch. In this warm, safe place the joey attaches itself to one of the two teats. The joey remains in the pouch for the first six to seven months of its life, feeding on its mother's milk.

This tiny, hairless joey is around 6 to 7 weeks old. You can see that its claws are long and sharp already.

When the joey is around five to six months old, it begins to peep out of the pouch and feed on pap which its mother produces at that time. Pap is a form of koala droppings. It is rich, soft and runny and full of the **bacteria** that the joey will soon need to digest its **diet** of eucalyptus leaves.

This joey grips tightly to its mother's fur when riding on her back. Once it starts feeding on leaves, the joey will start to grow in size much more quickly.

Out of the pouch

The joey gradually spends more time out of the pouch and begins to eat fresh leaves. At nine months old it weighs about one kilogram and is finally too big to fit inside the pouch. It rides on its mother's back for much of the time and in cold or wet weather it clings to her belly to sleep. The joey feeds on its mother's milk until it is about a year old. Because it is too large for the pouch, it puts its head inside it to suckle.

The young koala remains with its mother until the next season's joey comes out of the pouch. At this point it is time for the older joey finally to leave its mother.

Koala inbreeding

Once they have left their mothers, some young koalas travel up to 50 kilometres (30 miles) to join new koala groups elsewhere. If there are none within reach of these young, wandering koalas, they may be forced to stay and breed with animals in their own group. This can eventually result in what is called **inbreeding**, which can lead to the group being more likely to catch diseases and have other serious health problems. Some isolated koala **populations** in South Australia and Victoria have become inbred.

Land clearing and tree dieback

Since the arrival of the European settlers in the 18th century, around 80 per cent of the **native** eucalyptus forest has been destroyed in Australia. Settlers have farmed and built their towns mainly on the rich lands along the east coast, cutting down trees to make space for themselves and their activities. However these are some of the areas where many koalas live because they like the trees that grow on the fertile soils there.

Threatened!

As well as koalas, these other species are threatened by land clearing in Australia:

- Red goshawk
- Glossy black cockatoo
- Swift parrot
- Leadbeater's possum
- Grey-headed flying fox.

Eucalyptus forests continue to be cleared to make way for houses, farmland, mines, shops, factories and roads, as well as for the timber industry. The rate of land clearing in Australia is one of the highest in the world. In 2002 in the state of Queensland alone, 75,000 hectares of **bush** was destroyed. That is an area equal to one tenth the size of Tasmania.

Land clearing can directly kill koalas since some animals fall to the ground when the trees are being chopped down. Those that survive may be forced to move from their **home ranges**. When this happens they are more at risk from being run over by traffic or attacked by dogs. Establishing new home ranges can be difficult or impossible and can lead to overcrowding. Stress caused by a lack of suitable **habitat** and a shortage of food can weaken some koalas and make them more likely to catch diseases.

A bulldozer clears forest land to make way for new houses in north Queensland. Fewer trees mean less food and shelter for koalas.

Tree dieback causes trees to die rapidly, often in large numbers like these. Although it is becoming more common in rural areas, dieback can be prevented by good farming techniques.

Sometimes when a forest is logged, only some trees are removed. Even this can be very harmful since these may be important food trees for koalas living in the area. Their removal may mean the forest can no longer support its koala **population**.

Dieback

Large-scale land clearing has led to patches of remaining forest being separated by large areas of land without trees. Small, scattered islands of forest are more likely to suffer from further harmful changes in the **environment**. Trees help bind the soil with their roots and without trees soil can be worn away by wind and water and important **nutrients** may be washed out. Rising water levels underground and the build-up of salts in the soil are other common problems. These can all cause the gradual death of the trees that remain. This is known as tree dieback and is creating serious problems for koalas and other animals that live in the remaining woodlands.

Bushfires

Fire is a natural part of the cycle of life in the dry Australian **bush**, particularly in the summer months. If there were no fires at all a few fast-growing trees and undergrowth plants would take over and a great variety of other plant **species** would be lost. Controlled fires keep undergrowth down and allow some of the slower-growing trees to grow.

Aborigines probably carried out regular burning of forests and grasslands for thousands of years but they were careful to keep their fires under control. Since European settlers arrived, the number of bushfires has risen sharply, leading to widespread damage to wildlife and the **environment**.

▲ Bushfires like this one can have natural causes, such as lightning strikes. They can also be started accidentally by sparks from barbecues or cigarettes thrown into the grass. Sadly, some people even begin fires deliberately.

Burning up

The intense bushfires around Sydney in January 2002 occurred during a drought and were one of the worst natural disasters to hit New South Wales for a century. These fires had a disastrous effect on koalas and other wildlife. Very few animals survived the fires which lasted for around three weeks. Now that this area of bush is much reduced, it is more likely to be seriously damaged by large, intense fires in future.

Eucalyptus trees have **adapted** to cope with flames and within just a few weeks of a fire, many will start to regrow. If much of the tree has been destroyed, new shoots may still appear from the **lignotuber** below ground. However, if the trees lose all their leaves by fire two or three times in a few years, they are not likely to survive.

Fire and water

Moisture **evaporates** from the leaves of plants and later falls as rain. The more the land is cleared of trees and bush, the less it rains, and the risks of drought and fire become greater still.

Amazingly, eucalyptus trees can often survive bushfires. Here you can see new shoots sprouting from a eucalypt blackened by a recent bushfire.

Impact on koalas

Bushfires are now a major threat to koalas because much of their **habitat** is so broken up. Small, isolated koala **populations** can easily be wiped out by a single bushfire.

After the fire has died down, koalas' paws can easily be burnt when they come to the ground to move to another tree. Because there is less ground cover after a fire, koalas are also more at risk from **predators** such as dogs. Many often starve as their food supply can take several weeks to re-grow.

Koala predators

Koalas come to the ground regularly to move between trees. They walk quite awkwardly but can run if they have to. They are particularly vulnerable to attack from predators when they are on the ground like this.

Koalas have only a few **predators** that are **native** to Australia. These include goannas (a type of large, tree-climbing lizard), dingoes, wedge-tailed eagles, large owls and pythons, but they are not a serious threat to the survival of koala **populations**. Today, the biggest predator threat to koalas comes from domestic dogs which are not native to Australia, but have been **introduced** by humans.

Domestic dogs

Thousands of koalas are killed each year by pet dogs. This is a particular problem in suburban areas where dogs are more common and trees more scattered. Trees cover only a small percentage of suburban land, so for koalas to find enough to eat, their **home ranges** need to cover a large area. As a result, they have to spend more time on the ground going from one food tree to the next, putting them more at risk from dog attacks.

Usually attacks occur at night when koalas are most active. Even dogs in fenced gardens with no trees are a threat, because koalas can climb most fences and often need to cross gardens to reach eucalyptus trees nearby. Koala skin is soft with very little fat underneath and just one quick dog bite may be enough to kill. Even if the koala appears to survive, it may die later from shock or infection.

Introduced predators

There are many animals from other countries that have been brought to Australia since European settlement. Some were introduced deliberately to the wild, while others came by accident or have escaped from zoos and homes. These **feral** animals have had a disastrous impact in Australia, affecting the country's economy and its wildlife and plants.

Introduced **species** often do not have natural predators in their new country, so their populations increase and spread rapidly. The native wildife has not evolved to cope with the foreign invaders and eventually the introduced animals take the place of the native species. The European red fox, for instance, was brought to Australia by settlers in the mid-19th century. The foxes spread quickly and are now found on most of the mainland. Attacks by foxes are threatening the survival of many native species, such as the numbat, a termite-eating **marsupial**. Although not a big threat to koalas, red foxes may occasionally attack young koalas when their mother comes to the ground to move between trees.

Cat dangers

Large feral cats can occasionally attack and kill young koalas and they have had a devastating effect on Australia's smaller native wildlife.

This young bird is a wedge-tailed eagle. Native to Australia, these birds are one of the world's largest eagles. Their **prey** includes rabbits, hares, snakes, lizards and occasionally young koalas.

By the early 20th century koalas had become **extinct** in South Australia as a result of the fur trade. In the 1920s around eighteen koalas were **introduced** to Kangaroo Island, which lies just off the south coast. Although koalas had never before lived on the island, introducing them seemed a good idea as people thought they would be safe from **predators** there.

One of the scientists who helped introduce koalas to Kangaroo Island was Professor Wood Jones. Here he releases the first koala on to the island in 1923.

Since then most of the forest has been cleared from Kangaroo Island to make way for open farmland and a large sheep **population**. The small areas of woodland that are left do not have a chance to grow because the young trees are continually eaten by sheep.

Overcrowded

Because there is no opportunity for koalas from other populations to reach the island, the koalas here are now suffering from **inbreeding**. The introduced koalas did not have the chlamydia **bacterium** that acts as a natural population control, so their numbers have been increasing too fast. The latest koala survey in 2001 estimated that there were between 21,000 and 33,000 koalas on the island (although not all scientists agree that the numbers are so high). What is known for sure is that the koalas on Kangaroo Island are now very overcrowded. There are too few trees where young koalas can set up their own **home ranges** and they are steadily munching their way through a limited supply of eucalyptus leaves, destroying the **habitat** of other threatened **species**. This situation is an example of how intervention by humans can upset the balance of nature.

Although koala numbers are falling fast elsewhere in Australia, they are increasing too fast on Kangaroo Island and some other isolated areas in Victoria. There is now a hot debate over what to do about these overcrowded populations. While some scientists agree that the problem comes from the lack of trees, others think there are too many koalas and that they should be shot on a large scale to reduce the population. This idea has been rejected by the government partly because koalas now attract many high-spending foreign tourists to the island.

Artificial birth control is one method that has been used to try and reduce the number of koalas on the island. So far almost 3500 animals on the island have been sterilized (so they can no longer breed) and released back into the wild. Around 1200 of these have now been relocated to the mainland. However, not all scientists agree with this solution.

Koalas are now overcrowded on Kangaroo Island. These two koalas are sitting in a eucalypt that has been stripped of its leaves in places. Too many koalas living in too few trees means less food for all the species that live in these woodlands.

What can be done?

To solve the overcrowding problem on Kangaroo Island some **conservationists** want to:
· create more habitat for koalas by restoring eucalyptus forest
· protect young trees from sheep and rabbits by fencing
· link koala woodlands by planting trees between them, forming corridors through which koalas can move freely.

Over 100 **mammal**, bird and plant **species** have become **extinct** in Australia since the arrival of European settlers over 200 years ago. Many of these species lived nowhere else in the world. The Tasmanian tiger, for example, was a meat-eating **marsupial** that looked similar to a wolf. Because it **preyed** on the settlers' livestock it was hunted down and killed until the last-known animal died in 1936.

What koalas need

How can koalas survive the impact of human activities? Koalas need safe areas of undisturbed **habitat** and other koalas nearby to interact with. If an area is built up with houses, roads, car parks and back yards, koalas find it more difficult to establish **home ranges**. Without these they can die from lack of food and shelter. Swimming pools in people's back yards are also dangerous. Although they can swim, some koalas drown because they can't climb out if they fall in.

Road building

When people build new roads through koala habitat, the effects can be disastrous. Koalas may only be able to reach all the trees in their home range by crossing and re-crossing roads. Fast-moving cars pose one of the greatest risks to koalas.

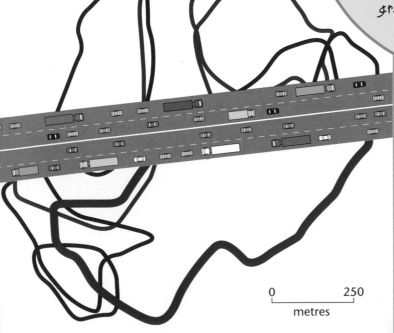

0   250
metres

This diagram shows what happens to koala home ranges if a road is built through them. The new road breaks up the group and means koalas have to face the constant danger of busy traffic in order to move around. It also destroys home trees and means they have less food to eat.

This is a road on the Koala Beach Estate. You can see the road signs that encourage drivers to slow down and also the trees that have been planted around the estate to help the koalas feel more at home.

A koala-friendly housing estate

On the north coast of New South Wales local people, koala researchers and a property company have joined up to create the first koala-friendly housing **development**. It is called the Koala Beach Estate.

The site already had a **population** of koalas. The researchers fitted each koala here with a collar and a **radio transmitter**. This was used to find out how koalas were using the site (where their favourite trees were, how the koalas moved about, and so on). Every home tree used by the koalas was identified and recorded, and these were preserved when the houses were built.

Dogs and cats are banned from the estate. Many people don't mind this and are keen to buy a house on an estate with koalas. Traffic is slowed down by speed humps on the road and other speed restrictions. More koala food trees have been planted and swimming pools fitted with ropes so koalas can climb out if they fall in. Fences on the estate also have gaps at the bottom to allow koalas and other **native** animals to pass freely underneath.

Several years after the development began it appears to be a success. Koalas and other threatened species such as blossom bats and glossy black cockatoos, still survive on the estate alongside the human residents.

Koalas are a protected **species**, which means that people cannot take them from the wild or have them in their possession without a special permit. It also means koalas cannot be kept as pets. However, although these laws exist to protect koalas themselves, they fail to protect the eucalyptus woodlands where they live, and without eucalyptus trees there would be no koalas.

NO TREE... NO ME!

Australian Koala Foundation

Conservation campaigns such as this one aim to make the public more aware of the threats that koalas are facing today.

Listing koalas

At present it is up to each state government in Australia to protect its koalas and to list their 'status'. The status of a **species** reflects how close people think it is to actually dying out. The listings generally range from common (or not thought to be under threat) through threatened, vulnerable and rare to endangered and then, finally **extinct**. The nearer to extinction a species is listed, the more a government is responsible for **conserving** both the species and its **habitat**. Different states have different approaches to listing their koalas: in Queensland, koalas are currently listed as common, in New South Wales as vulnerable, in South Australia as rare and in Victoria they are not listed at all.

National Koala Act

Conservationists are calling on the Australian Government for a National Koala Act, or for changes to existing law, that will help ensure the long-term future of koalas. They want the law to:

· list the koala as a 'threatened species'. This could lead to an official National Recovery Plan for koalas
· fully protect privately owned koala habitat by offering tax benefits to landholders who protect habitat on their land
· ensure that when any land is to be cleared, there must first be an investigation to see if it is koala habitat. If it is, then clearing the land must not be allowed.

Eighty per cent of koala habitat has already been lost and most that remains is on privately owned land where the pressure to clear and develop land is increasing as the human **population** grows. More than ever, there is now an urgent need for national laws that protect both koalas and their woodlands over the whole of their **distribution**.

In 2000, the koala was listed as threatened under the US Endangered Species Act, which will help to raise awareness around the world of the koala's situation. Koalas joined other non-US species on this list, such as chimpanzees and tigers.

A flagship species

The koala has been called a flagship species. This means that because it is familiar to people all over the world, it can be used to promote the need for the conservation of Australia's eucalyptus woodlands. Other threatened animals and plants also depend on these woodlands. Because the koala is so appealing, people are more likely to want to save its habitat. This would help other species that use the same habitat, too.

These grey-headed flying foxes are a kind of bat. They live and roost in large numbers in eucalyptus woodland and are one of the many species that would be helped if koala habitat were better protected by law.

In 1994 an ambitious project to find and map koala **habitats** in eastern Australia was started. The project is called the Koala Habitat Atlas and is being run by an organization called the Australian Koala Foundation.

Scientists are examining remaining areas of eucalyptus woodland and working out how suitable they are as koala habitat. The Atlas shows where good koala habitat occurs even when there are no koalas living there at present. The Atlas is not an actual book of maps, but a collection of important data on a computer.

Australian Koala Foundation (AKF)

The AKF is a non-government scientific research organization set up in 1986 by two people who were worried about the threats to koalas. Its main aim is to help **conserve** and manage koalas in the wild and make sure their future is secured. The foundation provides money for research in order to learn more about koalas and to find out the best ways of protecting them. Another important area of their work is education and they provide information for teachers and students and others interested in the welfare of koalas.

These two scientists are from the Australian Koala Foundation. One is measuring a tree while the other is searching for koala droppings to find out if this is a koala's home tree.

A long way to go

Koalas are living in areas spread over more than one million square kilometres (620,000 square miles). By 2003 the Atlas had surveyed over 50,000 individual trees from around 1200 sites. This sounds quite a lot, but in fact this is around only 5 per cent of the entire area it will eventually map. The first areas that were completed include those where koalas are most at risk.

So far, the results paint a sorry picture. Much of the existing koala habitat is now very broken up and of poor quality. There are also thousands of hectares of suitable habitat that no longer have healthy koala **populations** in them.

A scientist gives this wild koala a health check while undertaking research for the Koala Habitat Atlas.

Using the Atlas

In Australia, most decisions about the use of land — **development** for roads, factories or houses — are made by town planners and local authorities who often have little understanding of the needs of koalas or habitat conservation. With the information from the Atlas, the Australian Koala Foundation is working with town planners, as well as local communities and landowners, to help plan a more secure future for koalas.

Can tourism help koalas?

The tourism industry in Australia has been growing rapidly over recent years and is now very important to the country's economy. Many foreign tourists come to see Australia's unique and fascinating wildlife. The koala is one of the country's best known animals and plays an important role as a symbol promoting Australia's tourism industry. Photos and cartoons of koalas are often used in advertisements and travel brochures designed to attract tourists.

Koalas are big business

Income from foreign tourists who come to see koalas totalled around £420 million in 1996 and was expected to rise to over £800 million by 2000. This includes money spent by tourists on wildlife tours in the **bush**, visiting zoos and wildlife parks, accommodation, photographs with koalas and souvenirs. Koalas bring in far more money each year than, for example, Australia's woodchip industry, which is responsible for some of the tree clearing and koala **habitat** destruction (the export of woodchips earned Australia £315 million in 1999-2000).

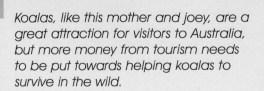

Koalas, like this mother and joey, are a great attraction for visitors to Australia, but more money from tourism needs to be put towards helping koalas to survive in the wild.

Tourists get close to a koala in the bush to take a photograph. This one is on Kangaroo Island.

Can ecotourism help koalas?

Despite their importance to tourism, koalas have not benefited very much from it. Little of the money brought in by tourists has so far been put back into **conserving** them or their habitat.

However, things are beginning to change and more tourists now want to see koalas and other wildife in their natural **environment**. As a result, special holidays called ecotours are becoming popular. Ecotourism means enjoying nature and learning about living things and the environment by experiencing it. Real ecotourism supports wildlife conservation, benefits local people and does little harm to the environment.

On a koala ecotour, local guides take visitors out to find, observe, photograph and enjoy koalas in the wild. These educational tours may last between two and fourteen days. Most people love seeing koalas in their natural environment, and the challenge of finding them in the wild adds to the excitement. Some ecotours give people the chance to help with practical conservation projects, such as planting koala food trees. Ecotourism can really help koalas because of practical help such as this. The money from ecotours goes into further research and more conservation projects.

More koalas are living in the suburbs because their **habitat** is shrinking. Attacks by dogs and accidents with cars mean that the number of koalas in care is rising. Many local groups of people across Australia look after thousands of sick, injured or orphaned animals each year and some vets give their skills and time free of charge. In a few places there are hospitals just for koalas. The Koala Hospital in Port Macquarie, New South Wales, for example, looks after between 150 and 200 koalas each year. Up to 90 koalas are cared for at any one time.

This is what happens at the hospital during the course of a normal working day:

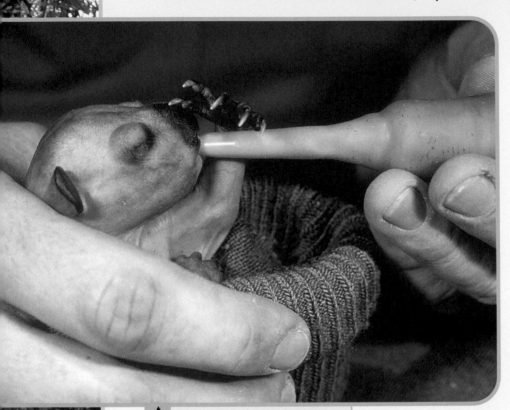

Specially trained carers look after sick or injured koalas. Orphaned joeys need constant care. Cosy in its woollen 'pouch' this tiny infant, is given some milk by a carer.

5a.m. Specially trained people called 'leaf pickers' set out in a truck to pick fresh leaves for the koala patients. Leaf pickers know a lot about the different types of eucalypts and they have to find and pick the right kind of leaves for each koala in the hospital! This is becoming difficult as more eucalyptus trees are being cut down in the area.

7a.m. Back at the hospital, staff separate the different leaves into piles and put them in cold water to keep them fresh. Some koalas can't eat properly because of injuries to their jaw, so their leaves are chopped up. Meanwhile, the koala patients that have been active during the night now go to sleep for the day.

9a.m. onwards Staff start work in the office. They keep as quiet as possible because the koalas are sleeping. During the day, schoolchildren and other groups visit the hospital to learn about how the koala patients are looked after and what sort of problems they will face when they are released again into the wild.

4p.m. Because koalas are **nocturnal**, their day begins at sunset when they start waking up. Staff now give them plenty of eucalyptus leaves to munch for the night. Sick koalas are given medicines and any bandages are checked or changed.

5p.m. onwards This can be a busy time for the hospital because more sick and injured koalas may be brought in. Catching koalas safely when they are upset or hurt is a skilled job. As well as capturing them, staff have to make a careful note of the types of trees in the area — so koalas can be given the correct leaves to eat back at the hospital.

This koala is receiving some medicine during its stay in hospital. Once recovered, it is essential that koalas are returned to a safe and undamaged habitat. If they are not, they are very likely to return to hospital injured or sick, or may even die in the wild.

Lone Pine Koala Sanctuary in Queensland started the first collection of koalas in captivity in 1927. With over 130 koalas, it now has the world's largest number of these animals. Zoos across the world have koalas and San Diego Zoo in the USA has the largest collection of them outside Australia. This is partly because they are able to grow the right kind of eucalyptus for their koalas.

Keeping koalas

Koalas are not easy to keep in captivity because they are such fussy feeders. In the past it has also been difficult to breed koalas in captivity, although there are now some successful breeding programmes. San Diego Zoo has bred over 100 koalas since 1976, for instance. Although it now has a very healthy **population** of koalas, the zoo regularly tries to get new animals from Australia to make sure that its koala collection doesn't suffer from **inbreeding**.

In 1998, Lone Pine Koala Sanctuary announced the birth of the world's first **marsupial** using artificial insemination. Artificial insemination means introducing **sperm** from a male to a female by non-natural means to make her **pregnant**. The koala joey was called Lica and her birth and survival were the result of four years of research. This method of breeding is more difficult in marsupials than other **mammals** because of how their bodies work, but it could be better for koalas in zoos as there is no need to move males around by road or air to meet females for mating. The success of koala breeding programmes is helping to develop similar methods for other threatened marsupials, such as the endangered northern hairy-nosed wombat.

Koalas are popular with people all over the world. People love having their photograph taken with them.

Can zoos help?

Koalas are enormously popular with zoo visitors. Zoos around the world play a valuable role in raising awareness about the threats faced by koalas and the importance of their **conservation**. Zoos also make it possible for thousands of people to see live koalas, an experience that many may not be able to have in the wild.

What about the future?

Although koala breeding in captivity is successful it cannot help the long-term conservation of these animals because koalas bred in zoos can't survive if they are released into the wild. In addition, zoos do not play a large part in the conservation of koala **habitats**. The only real future for koalas lies in protecting wild koalas and their natural surroundings.

A few zoos carry out research into koala conservation and some provide money for research and surveys. For instance when San Diego Zoo lends its koalas to another zoo, in exchange for receiving the koalas, the borrowing zoo must put some money directly towards koala conservation in Australia.

The future for koalas

There are good reasons to be hopeful about the future for koalas. They are Australia's most loved animal and are recognized worldwide as a symbol for the country. They are also closely linked with Australia's expanding tourism industry.

Many people are now working hard to help **conserve** koalas, from the national koala conservation group to local groups, individuals and koala hospitals. Public awareness of the problems koalas face is increasing in Australia and throughout the world. However more than popularity is needed to save these animals!

The Koala **Habitat** Atlas is helping to provide land-use planners with much needed information on suitable koala habitat. Decisions on koala habitat conservation should be more informed and effective as a result and this should lead to great improvements in koala conservation.

Koalas are unique and unmistakable animals and many people see them as a powerful symbol of Australia.

koalas and Aborigines

Although koalas were once hunted for food by the Aborigines, this is no longer permitted. However, koalas are important in Aboriginal culture. For instance, some Aborigines believe that it is forbidden to break the koala's bones if they kill one. Although they were permitted to eat the animals, they were not allowed to skin them, and they always treated the koala's body with respect. The Aborigines believed that if they did not, there was a danger that all the water in the land would dry up, and there would be a terrible drought.

While koalas inhabiting the suburbs are often at risk, plans made especially for koalas at the Koala Beach Estate in New South Wales so far show that koalas can survive when living close to people. At the same time, the people on the estate are hugely proud of 'their' koalas. This inspiring example of koalas and people living well together could be a model for housing **developments** elsewhere in Australia.

The Australian Koala Foundation is pressing the government for stronger laws that will protect habitat for koalas. Landholders need encouragement to conserve eucalyptus woodlands for koalas on their land. Listing koalas as a nationally threatened **species** would strengthen measures to conserve koalas wherever they live in the wild.

The koala as teacher

'I think that the koala is a powerful symbol for conservation and a great teacher. It has the potential to teach us how to better manage our land and our forests, and many other things.'

Deborah Tabart, Australian Koala Foundation

Research into wild koalas is essential for their conservation. These scientists are carefully measuring the size of a young joey's head. Information like this is used to learn more about koalas and how they live.

How can you help?

Koalas need help if they are to survive in the wild. Even though their problems are very serious, there are many ways that you can help.

First of all, you can learn more about koalas and their **conservation** by looking up information on the web and reading books. You can take part in a foster-a-koala scheme like the one run by the Australian Koala Foundation, where you can sponsor a captive koala at a wildlife sanctuary. By doing this you will be helping to raise money to save koalas in the wild.

What about raising some money for charities working for koala conservation? You could hold a koala disco and charge an entry fee, or sell items on a stall — for example cakes, biscuits, koala cards or gift tags you have made, or goods from one of the koala charities.

In Australia

If you live in Australia (or are just visiting), you can take part in Save the Koala Month. This event is held each July and aims to raise funds and awareness and to inspire people to do something positive for koalas.

Dogs are a problem for koalas. If you have a dog make sure it does not harm or play with koalas. At night keep your dog indoors and not outside in your back yard. When watching koalas remember to do so from a distance so that you do not disturb them.

These school children are from Brisbane. They are raising money for koalas during Save the Koala month by doing a sponsored walk through the large koala woodland that lies next to their school.

If there are koalas living near you be aware of any threats to them. You can help by joining your local wildlife or koala group too. There may be opportunities for you to get involved in active conservation work for koalas. If you have a swimming pool, make sure there is a sturdy rope fixed in it so koalas can climb out if they fall in. If you plant food trees for koalas, make sure they are away from busy roads or swimming pools.

If you are concerned about what may be happening to koalas, speak up for them. Writing a letter to your local newspaper can be very effective in making people in your district more aware of koalas and the importance of their conservation.

When travelling by car, make sure your family always carries a sack, blanket, towel or box in case you find an injured koala by the roadside.
If you do find a koala in trouble contact your local koala or wildlife rescue group, or koala hospital. Be careful! Koalas have sharp teeth and claws and can inflict a nasty wound if they are frightened.

Write away!

Whatever you do for koalas, write to the Australian Koala Foundation and tell them all about it. It encourages them to work even harder for koalas if they know you love koalas too, and they may well publish news of your good work on their website.

adaptation   way in which a living thing adjusts to its surroundings

ancestor   distant relative that lived a very long time ago

bacterium   single-cell organism found almost everywhere; some cause disease. More than one are called bacteria.

bush   uncultivated area usually covered in trees and shrubs

conservationist   person who works in conservation

conserve   protect wild plants, animals and their habitats for the future; conservation is the work done to protect these things

development   what humans do to change the natural landscape, including the building of houses, roads and factories

diet   food a creature eats

digestive system   part of the body where food is broken down and absorbed into the bloodstream

distribution   geographical area in which an animal or plant occurs

environment   all the factors (physical, chemical and biological) that affect a living thing

evaporate   turn from liquid into vapour

evolve   undergo gradual change over a long period of time

extinct   no longer in existence

feral   animal that has become wild

fibre   roughage in food that needs a lot of digesting

fossil   plant or animal, or impression of a plant or animal, preserved in rock

habitat   place an animal lives in, such as a desert, river, or rainforest

home range   area in which an animal normally lives or travels over in search of food

inbreeding   producing young by breeding with animals that are closely related. Some isolated populations of koalas are now inbred.

introduce   bring species to a new area where they are not native

lignotuber   large, woody, bulbous underground structure containing water, at the base of a eucalyptus tree

mammal   warm-blooded animal with fur that feeds its young with milk from its body

marsupial   type of mammal that gives birth to tiny, under-developed young that usually live in their mother's pouch for the early part of their life

native   belonging to a particular country or place

nocturnal   active at night

nutrient   substance that provides nourishment

pollinate   transfer pollen from the flowers of one plant to another and make the plant produce seeds

population   group of living things of the same species within a particular area

predator   animal that hunts or kills another animal for food

pregnant   expecting young

prey   hunt or kill another animal for food. The prey is also the animal that is hunted.

radio transmitter   tiny radio attached to animals in the wild that gives out signals so scientists can detect where they are

rainforest   ancient, mature forest in an area where there is heavy rainfall

species   particular type of animal or other living thing

sperm   male reproductive cell which joins with an egg produced by a female to form a new living creature

subspecies   population of animals or other living things that differs slightly from others of the same species. Subspecies are usually restricted to a particular geographical area. For example, there are thought to be two subspecies of koala, the northern koala and the southern koala.

territory   personal space defended by an animal or group of animals. It usually contains areas of safety and shelter and sources of food.

toxin   poisonous substance

tropical   area lying close to the equator where the climate is moist and very warm

Conservation groups and websites

All the organizations below are working to help protect koalas or their habitat. You can find out more about them by visiting their websites.

Australian Koala Foundation
www.savethekoala.com
Chief non-government organization in Australia working for the conservation of koalas and their habitat. Runs fostering schemes for adult koalas and joeys and is responsible for the Koala Habitat Atlas project. Lively, informative website.

Australian Government: Department of the Environment and Heritage
www.deh.gov.au
The Department of the Environment and Heritage advises the Australian Government on policies for the protection and conservation of the environment. Their large website covers a wide range of subjects from threatened species and pollution to climate change in Australia.

Worldwide Fund for Nature Australia
www.wwf.org.au
International charity that takes action to conserve threatened species, tackle global threats to the environment and seek sustainable solutions for the benefit of people and nature. It has branches in many countries around the world. The Australian branch campaigns for the protection of native forests.

Books

A Photographic Guide to Mammals of Australia, Ron Strahan
(New Holland, 1998)

Australian Mammals, Leonard Cronin (Envirobook, 2000)

Green Guide to Mammals of Australia, Terence Lindsey
(New Holland, 1998)

Koalas, Vincent Serventy and Carol Serventy (New Holland, 2002)

Living Things: Adaptation, Holly Wallace (Heinemann Library, 2001)

Living Things: Survival and Change, Steve Parker (Heinemann
Library, 2000)

Nature Files: Animal Homes, Anita Ganeri (Heinemann Library, 2003)

The Koala, Roger Martin and Kathrine Handasyde (Krieger, 1999)

The Koala Book, Ann Sharp (Australian Koala Foundation, Pelican,
1995)

Videos

Wild Down Under, narrated by Matt Day (BBC, 2003)

CD-ROMs

Mammals of Australia, (Natural Learning Pty Ltd, 1999)

Index

Titles in the *Animals under Threat* series include:

Hardback   0 431 18902 1

Hardback   0 431 18903 X

Hardback   0 431 18904 8

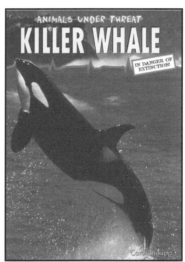

Hardback   0 431 18905 6

Hardback   0 431 18906 4

Hardback   0 431 18907 2

Find out about the other titles in this series on our website www.heinemann.co.uk/library